# SANDWICH POETS

# DOLPHINS LEAP LAMPPOSTS

## DAVE CALDER
## ERIC FINNEY
### and
## IAN SOUTER

Illustrated by
**Jane Eccles**

MACMILLAN CHILDREN'S BOOKS

First published 2002
by Macmillan Children's Books
a division of Macmillan Publishers Limited
20 New Wharf Road, London N1 9RR
Basingstoke and Oxford
www.panmacmillan.com

Associated companies throughout the world

ISBN 0 330 48360 9

Eric Finney: 'I Can See You Now' first published in *Senses Poems*, 'Six Riddles' and '57 Varieties' first
published in *Billy and Me and a Cowboy in Black*, Edward Arnold; 'Left Out Together' and 'Boy on the
Beach' first published in *Our Side of the Playground*, The Bodley Heady; 'Snail' first published in *Billy and
Me and the Igloo*, Edward Arnold; 'City Fan' first published in *Football Fever*, Oxford; 'An Alien Limerick'
first published in *Loopy Limericks*, Harper Collins; 'Best-of-all-Festival' first published in *The School Year*,
Macmillan; 'Our Solar System' first published in *Spaceways*, Oxford; 'Haiku/Highcoo/Hicuckoo!' first
published in *This Poem Doesn't Rhyme*, Viking; 'Just a Small War' first published in *Shorts*, Macmillan.

# CONTENTS

## Dave Calder

# Eric Finney

# Ian Souter

# Dave Calder

At school, Dave Calder's best subjects were English and Daydreaming. In fact, it was his English teacher who suggested that he could make a career of Daydreaming. His favourite position for working is flat on his back in warm sunshine, but since he lives in Glasgow he has to use a sofa most of the year. His family, who are scientists or possibly part of his daydreams, find it difficult to believe he is working flat out with his eyes shut.

# Desk

It was stuffy in the classroom.
He put his hand inside his desk,
feeling for a pencil. It was cool in there,
he let his hand swing aimlessly around.
The space within seemed vast, and when
he reached in further he found
nothing, could feel no books, no ruler.
His hand floated as if in a bath of shadows,
airy and refreshing, not at all
the same place that the rest of him was in.

He put both hands in, let them drift
deeper, this way and that. It was more than empty,
the inside had no sides. His hands
never reappeared through some unexpected hole.
He lifted the lid quietly a little more. A waft
of soft air cooled his face, the same
as on summer nights or under leafy trees.

He bent his head down to the gap. He looked inside.
Dark as deep water, deep as a clear night sky.
He smiled. He put his head inside.
'What are you doing?' asked the teacher. But he didn't hear.
He slid his shoulders in, and then
before anyone could reach to stop him,
he bent from the waist, kicking his chair back,
and with a muffled cry of pleasure
dived. For a split second,
as the room filled with fresh air,
we watched his legs slide slowly down into the desk
and disappear. And then the lid fell back,
shut, with a soft thud.

# Greengrocer

I went into the greengrocer's:
the vegetables and the fruit
were all piled neatly in their boxes
and a large watermelon lay in the corner.

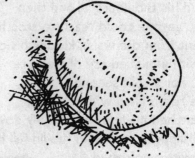

I couldn't see the greengrocer.
The shop smelt ripe and drowsy. I put
three bananas in a paper bag. It was
so still and silent I felt watched.
The mushrooms looked like knee bones.
The watermelon lay contented in the corner.

What had happened to the greengrocer?
I took some carrots. I stuffed
plastic bags with spinach,
with the long green teeth of okra,
with courgettes like tiny truncheons.
The watermelon lay big-bellied in the corner.

There was no sign of the greengrocer.
I called out, I waited, then I left
money by the till and went towards the door.
The enormous watermelon in the corner
snored.

# My Grandfather Gavin

My Grandfather Gavin
kept his Morris Minor
in a wooden boathouse
miles from the seashore,

but he drove it like
you'd steer a boat:
it bounced, bobbed and bellied,
only just afloat;

and up the rolling waves of hills
and down the other side
we sailed, as fast and thrilling
as a roller-coaster ride.

My Grandfather Gavin
was known near and far:
I think people stayed indoors
when he drove his car.

My Grandfather Gavin
had a round bald head —
it was rounder
and shinier
than his Morris Minor
and he parked it
in his bed.

# Stocking

The old long stockings – every year
their thick brown weave was stuffed
into stiffness, stretched
like a cartoon ostrich neck
with knobbly shapes – the parcels
to be teased out one by one with that intense
all-involving mix of hope and dread –
for who thinks on the past or future in
the moment of unwrapping the present?

So every year, starting with
the largest lumps stuck in the stocking's throat,
we'd work our way down, tunnelling
to find if fate matched our desires –
so difficult at seven in the morning
to praise the unwanted or expected,
to mask disappointment at the not quite right:

but life itself is a gift, even if it's
not just what we wanted,
and from gifts we learn to accept,
to understand at last that the real gift
was the stocking itself, year after year,
and the hands that filled it, and the certainty
that after everything or anything,
however hollow our fantasies proved,
we would always find, tucked in the toe,
a tangerine, an apple,
and a sixpence.

# Flood

The rain fell all night, beating on roofs
as dark and hunched as hills,
cascading uncontained into the street
in wind-curved waterfalls.

All night the rain fell, kept falling.
This morning, the street's a river:
cars founder and sink, while buses
crawl laden as ocean liners,

raise bow-waves so swollen they break
booming across the pavement,
where tossed at the tide's rising mark
seaweed tangles to litter;

and under the hedges and gates
fish shoal in the gleaming shallows,
and further out, through the channel
marked by wave-slapped traffic lights,

dolphins leap lampposts, and whales
surge and sound in the deep roads.

# Pyramid

P
EAK
PLACE
PROUDLY
PROVIDING
PRESTIGIOUS
PLUSH PRIVATE
PILED PENTHOUSE
PERFECTLY PLANNED
PANORAMIC POSITION
PART PAYMENT POSSIBLE
PAST PHARAOHS PREFERRED

# Cat

I have walked on the wall
and
have put my eye on the world
and
it had better behave itself.

I have slouched under the bushes
and have made the lumps of feather-covered cat-meat
jump up and down
waving their uneatable bits and squeaking stupidly.

I have found slow wriggly things in my earth
and have pulled them with my claws
but they are not much fun
and they are not good cat-meat.

I have sat on the flowers, to watch
the big animal that brings me cat-meat
dig holes in my earth
but it was not looking for the wriggly slimy
things that are not cat-meat.

It is not as intelligent as a cat,
it does not use its claws to dig
and has nothing to put into the hole
except a stalk of something.

Then it goes. I smell the stalks
and since they are not cat-meat
I stand on them, and dig in my earth
to make it more as I like it

and the big animal is back.
It is jumping up and down
like the feather-covered cat-meat
and waving its uneatable bits
and squeaking stupidly.

It is more useless than I'd thought –
for all the jumping and waving it has not managed
to leave the ground and float to the tip of a tree.

If it did not bring me cat-meat
I should certainly eat it.

# The Bluebottle Pantoum

The bluebottle is buzzing round the bathroom
as angry and irritated as I am
listening to its crazy one-note tune.
The window's open. Go on, scram!

As angry and as irritated as I am,
I'm trying to be helpful – look here, fly,
the window's open. Go on, scram!
Stop droning on and use your eyes.

I'm trying to be helpful – look here, fly
a little to the left, then up. And please
stop droning on and use your eyes.
Do I have to beg you on my knees?

A little left, then up and out. Please.
I'm getting close to a murder most foul.
Do I have to beg you? On my knees
my hands are clenched upon a heavy towel.

I'm getting close to a murder most foul
listening to its crazy one-note tune.
My hands are clenched upon a heavy towel.
The bluebottle is buzzing round the bathroom.

# The Ball Talks in its Changing Room

I'm the star really. I'm the one
the crowds have come to watch.
I don't let it worry me. Before the match
they check me carefully, make sure
I'm really fit. After all
I have to take more pressure
than the rest of them. And then
it's the usual jokes about
there being more hot air in
the commentators than in me,
and the ref puts his arm around
my shoulders and says he hopes
I'll have a good game, no need
for a substitute, and off we go
to lead the players out. No time
for second thoughts once we start:
I'm in the middle of it all the way
with everybody shouting for me,
cheering as I dodge around the tackles,
or slide out of reach of players
who just want to put the boot in.
The crowd is all for me, willing me on,
praying that I'll reach the net,
and when I do, roaring with delight.
I take it as my due. The lads are all right
but, when all's said and done, Desmond,
they'd be nothing without me.

## At the Zoo

The lions have dug deep burrows,
the snakes have coiled up in despair,
the crocodile has lost his smile,
the rhino is running scared.

The hippos are wearing crash helmets,
the camels have clumped off to grump,
the leopard is looking rather sick
his spots have changed to goosebumps.

The panther's turned pale with fear,
as white as the Arctic fox,
the elephants are trying hard
to disguise themselves as rocks.

The turtles are sheltering in their shells,
the seals have submerged out of sight
the giraffes are giggling nervously
the tigers tremble with fright.

The birds of prey are praying today
they've disappeared to the last feather,
all you can hear from the herd of red deer
is knobbly knees knocking together.

The keepers are locked in their office,
only one brave cockatoo
shrieks out a final warning:
4b have arrived at the zoo!

# Invasion

When the aliens landed on Earth
their mighty battle feet
spread out in formation
along the shoreline of a sea.

When the aliens landed on Earth
their commander stood on the shore
and claimed the planet. After all,
there was no resistance to their force.

When the aliens landed on Earth
a boy, stepping over a puddle,
squashed them all.

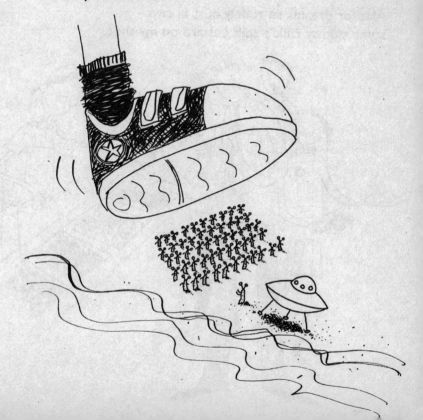

# The Amorous Teacher's Sonnet to His Love

Each morning I teach in a daze until
the bell that lets me hurry down and queue
with pounding heart to wait for you to fill
my eyes with beauty and my plate with stew.
Dear dinner lady, apple of my eye,
I long to shout I love you through the noise
and take your hand across the shepherd's pie
despite the squealing girls or snickering boys.
O let us flee together and start up
a little café somewhere in the Lakes
and serve day-trippers tea in china cups
and buttered scones on pretty patterned plates.

Alas for dreams so rudely bust in two –
some clumsy child's spilt custard on my shoe.

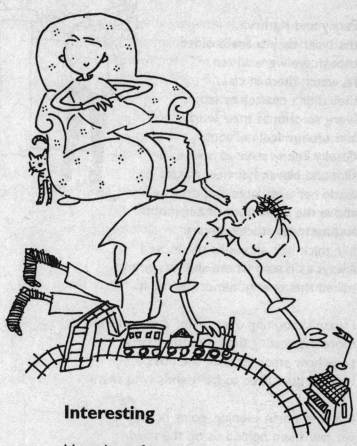

## Interesting

I have lots of interests —
my Lego, my train set,
my bike, my football.
My hobby is watching my dad
play with them all.

# Penny and Kathryn

Penny and Kathryn
that year they seemed older
though we were all ten.
I'd watch them in class,
they didn't chatter or laugh,
were so calm at their work
it made me feel nervous.
Gawky Penny seemed now to be
slim and clever, her new glasses
made her eyes large and dreamy
above the small pout of her mouth.
Kathryn was stocky, strong,
her thick hair shook as she moved
always as if sure where she was going:
I liked that energy, almost feared it.

I wasn't mooning over them, they were just
more interesting than the other girls,
somehow stronger than the boys.
I would have liked to be friends with them.

But one warm evening, going home,
we saw them behind us on the road,
two other boys and me, we said
let's hide, let's jump out, it's fun –
we thought it friendly, meant no harm.
And I hid behind a gate post like the others,
enjoying the wait, the tension,
and leapt up grinning, happy as a puppy,

but the girls didn't look surprised
or laugh or run or anything:
they just looked, and the looks
said they were past that sort of game,
that we were silly little boys, to be ignored,
and they left me standing foolish by the wall
feeling they were right and knowing
even as I made a rude face to cover up my shame
how big a gap there was between us
that I couldn't cross until I learnt
what different games would please them.

# Information for Travellers

As you read this poem you are on a spacecraft
travelling at sixty-six thousand miles an hour.
It spins as it flies: since you began to read
it has already turned nine miles to the east.
Be honest, you didn't feel a thing.
You are orbiting a star, not a very big one
compared to many of the ten thousand million others
that go round on the same galactic wheel,
and are flying at a height above its surface
of some ninety-three million miles.
We hope to cruise at this distance for another
eight thousand million years. What happens then
is anybody's guess. Despite its speed and size
this craft is a spacestation, a satellite, not designed
for interstellar flight. Its passengers
rely on the comfort of a pressurized cabin
to enjoy the voyage. We must advise you that,
in the event of collision, loss of atmosphere,
or any alteration in course which may result
in overheating or extreme cold, this craft is not
equipped with parachutes or emergency exits.
On a brighter note, the spaceship contains
an enormous variety of in-flight magazines,
meals to suit every taste, and enough
games, puzzles and adventures
to last a lifetime.
We hope you enjoy your voyage.
Thank you for flying Planet Earth.

## Alexander

King Alexander, third of Scotland,
really loved his wife a lot and
always tried to hurry home —
(This was long before the phone
was thought up by another Scot
called Alex, so the king could not
just call to say he'd been delayed
by work, bad weather or a plague)

So, one night in 1286, the king
(who'd got stuck in a council meeting
in Edinburgh) got on his horse
and, with a few friends of course
for kings are never alone,
set off to ride back to his home
to have his dinner with his wife
across the Firth of Forth in Fife.

A storm was rising. In the rain
they crossed the river. No train
was due for some six hundred years
so a boat took them (the ferry piers
are still there) and on the other shore
remounted and rode on once more —
travel in those days wasn't easy,
I'm sure that they were sore and queasy.

But Alex wouldn't hesitate:
he'd been king since he was eight,
survived rebellions and plots,
defeated invaders and got
back the Western Isles — he was not
going to let bad weather stop
him getting home in time for tea.
so on he galloped, recklessly.

It's not so far to Aberdour,
perhaps it took them half an hour,
but after that the darkness fell
and soon none of the men could tell
where they were. But the horses knew
and so they stumbled on. Just a few
miles before the castle at Kinghorn,
his queen, his dinner, a warm
fire and dry clothes, the king's good luck
ran out. In the dark fate struck.

His horse went the wrong way, and with
him on it, tumbled off a cliff.

Both dead. And in that moment history
changed completely. That one wrong turn
led to war, to Wallace, Bannockburn,
the Bruce, the Stewarts, all that came to be.

And Alexander never got his tea.

# On the Thirteenth Day of Christmas My True Love Phoned Me Up . . .

Well, I suppose I should be grateful, you've obviously gone
to a lot of trouble and expense – or maybe off your head.
Yes, I did like the birds – the small ones anyway were fun
if rather messy, but now the hens have roosted on my bed
and the rest are nested on the wardrobe. It's hard to sleep
with all that cooing, let alone the cackling of the geese
whose eggs are everywhere, but mostly in a broken smelly
heap
on the sofa. No, why should I mind? I can't get any peace
anywhere – the lounge is full of drummers thumping tom-
toms
and sprawling lords crashed out from manic leaping. The
kitchen is crammed with cows and milkmaids and smells of
a million stink bombs
and enough sour milk to last a year. The pipers? I'd
forgotten them –
they were no trouble, I paid them and they went. But I can't
get rid
of these young ladies. They won't stop dancing or turn the
music down
and they're always in the bathroom, squealing as they skid
across the flooded floor. No, I don't need a plumber round,
it's just the swans – where else can they swim? Poor things,
I think they're going mad, like me. When I went to wash my
hands one ate the soap, another swallowed the gold rings.
And the pear tree died. Too dry. So thanks for nothing,
love. Goodbye.

# Citizen of the World

when you are very small
maybe not quite born
your parents move
for some reason you may never understand they move
from their own town
from their own land
and you grow up in a place
that is never quite your home

and all your childhood people
with a smile or a fist say
you're not from here are you
and part of you says fiercely yes I am
and part of you feels no I'm not
I belong where my parents belonged

but when you go to their town, their country
people there also say
you're not from here are you
and part of you says no I'm not
and part of you feels fiercely yes I am

and so you grow up both and neither
and belong everywhere and nowhere much the same
both stronger and weaker for the lack of ground
able to fly but not to rest

and all over the world, though you feel alone
are millions like you, like a great flock of swallows
soaring or falling exhausted, wings beating the rhythm
of the wind that laughs at fences or frontiers,
whose home is itself, and the whole world it moves over.

# Changed

For months he taught us, stiff-faced.
His old tweed jacket closely buttoned up,
his gestures careful and deliberate.

We didn't understand what he was teaching us.
It was as if a veil, a gauzy bandage, got between
what he was showing us and what we thought we saw.

He had the air of a gardener, fussily protective
of young seedlings, but we couldn't tell
if he was hiding something or simply couldn't see it.

At first we noticed there were often scraps of leaves
on the floor where he had stood. Later, thin wisps
of thread like spider's web fell from his jacket.

Finally we grew to understand the work. And on that day
he opened his jacket, which to our surprise
seemed lined with patterned fabric of many shimmering
    hues.

Then he smiled and sighed. And with this movement
the lining rippled and instantly the room was filled
with a flickering storm of swirling butterflies.

# Eric Finney

Eric Finney lives with his wife in the lovely town of Ludlow in Shropshire. He occasionally manages to sneak away from lawn-mowing, house-painting, window-cleaning etc. to write poems in a cosy room lined with books, LPs and CDs. On visits to schools he particularly enjoys taking poetry assemblies. He is fond of walking and nearly always returns from walks with ideas for poems.

# A Funeral

The whole school came to the funeral.
Well, maybe not the cook,
But everybody else: dinner ladies,
Teachers, even Mr Morris, the headmaster,
And all the kids.
It was the first day back in September, see,
And we'd found this old hedgehog –
Blunted, bleached, dead –
In our scummy school pond.
It must have been there ages.
Mr Morris, on duty, said,
'It can't stay there. Use
Your initiative but not your fingers!'
What a pong as we heaved it out
Dripping on the caretaker's shovel,
All covered in waterweed.
And after lunch when Old Prickles
Was drained out, we fixed a funeral.
Miss found a clean black shoebox
For a coffin and we nailed
A piece of board between two poles
To carry it on.
Four of us each took the end of a pole
And we bore it down the field
To the Waste: it was very light.
The whole school fell in behind
In twos. There was no talking
And we all walked very slowly.
It was a funeral procession.
We put it in the hole we'd dug
And everybody gathered round to see.

'You say a prayer,' Ruth whispered.
So I said, 'This is a dead hedgehog.
We found it in the pond, God.'
It wasn't much to say
But I was a bit choked up.
I wasn't the only one either.

# I Can See You Now

When I first met
My blind friend Grace
She said, 'Will you please let me
Touch your face?'

I felt her gentle hands
Upon my skin:
She felt my lips and eyebrows
Then my nose and cheeks and chin.

Last of all she felt my hair
And gently held my head.
Then with a lovely smile:
'I can see you now,' she said.

# Left Out Together

There's the crowd of them again,
So happy and carefree,
Laughing and chatting, going somewhere,
Not including me.
They never say, 'Why don't you come too?'
I wander away and pretend I don't care –
But I do.

You look as though
You might be feeling the same:
Left on the sidelines,
Out of the game . . . ?
You are?
Well, I was wondering whether
We could team up
And both be left out together.

# Six Riddles

Head with a tail,
Each day plumper,
On the way
From jelly to jumper.

Space vehicle:
One of a fleet of nine.
This one, though,
Is yours and mine.

Water in disguise:
Three answers (no prize!)
This water's a stick;
This water's a star;
This water's so thick
You're not sure where you are.

Blow on me gently
To count the hours:
My parachutists
Plant new flowers.

You're Emperor, Conqueror, King,
You dead straight thing.

I'm highly placed
In a gang of ten:
A ring and above it
A ring again.

(Answers on p88)

# Just a Small War

We're watching the usual war pictures
On the six o'clock news on the box:
Shells exploding, bodies lying,
Fires, tanks, roadblocks.
Dave says, "Course, that's just a small war.
I'm not sure who's fighting who.
For *real* wars you have to go back
To World Wars One and Two.'

On the screen, in her shattered house,
A woman picks around for her stuff.

Bet she doesn't think it's a small war.
Bet she thinks it's real enough.

# Do Not Disturb

On Christmas Eve,
Under the window sill,
We found a chrysalis asleep,
Completely still.

Mum said, 'Don't disturb it.
It will fly one day.'
So we wished it
A Happy Chrysalis
And tiptoed quietly away.

# Snail

No knowing
Where you're going,
Slow tracker,
Backpacker;
You won't get
There just yet.

Easily seen
Where you've been.

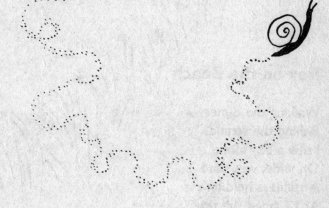

## Boy on the Beach

Walking the dunes
Behind the strand,
I saw a boy alone
On wide, wet sand.
A stillness held him
As he faced the tide,
Slowly raised his arms
Then spread them wide;
Stayed so for a minute
Then, breaking the spell,
Wrote large on the sand
With a stone or shell.
Walking on through marram grass
I soon could see:
He'd simply written
I AM ME.

# The Garden Next Door

Next door's garden
Is nothing but weeds.
Dad moans about getting
Their dandelion seeds.
There are three little kids:
They make mud pies,
Build dens in the bushes,
Chase butterflies.
They go mad with the dog,
Get their clothes all torn;
Our dad moans at their noise
As he trims the lawn.
We throw their dolls
And play balls back.
Our mum says
They're a rowdy pack.
Dad hoes his rows
And grumbles and glares,
But I wouldn't mind
A garden like theirs.

## City Fan

There's only one team for me.
My pals say it's a pity.
Well, I can't help that:
I support City.

Why don't you switch
To United, they say,
Spent millions on a striker
Only yesterday.

Or swap to Rangers –
They won the Cup;
Or Rovers: they're a team
On the up-and-up.

Rangers or Rovers . . .
Or even Athletic.
But City . . . well,
They're just pathetic.

Manager's terrible,
They're a hopeless lot.
And haven't they just
Lost ten on the trot?

It's all true what they say –
City do seem fated:
Ended up last season
Relegated.

I suppose it's all about
Loyalty.
I have this feeling
It's down to me.

It's Saturday. Raining.
Where's my anorak?
I'm off to see City.
They'll be back.

## 57 Varieties

It's a Heinz school ours;
If you want to know why it is
Well, we've got kids
In fifty-seven varieties:

'Cos we've got fighters
And lazy blighters,
Just a few posh kids,
Some not-enough-nosh kids,
Snotty kids, spotty kids,
A few really grotty kids,
First-in-the-queue kids,
Always-at-the-loo kids,

Scrappers, yappers,
Take a little nappers,
Nigglers, wrigglers,
Girlish gigglers,

Work-in-a-mess kids,
Couldn't-care-less-kids,
Schemers, dreamers,
Playground screamers,
Fibbers, cribbers,
Poke you in the ribbers,
Sad kids, sunny kids,
Dad's-got-pots-of-money kids;

There's clumsy clots,
Swankpots, swots,
Teacher's pets
(The weedy wets!),
Just-look-at-me kids,
Wouldn't-hurt-a-flea kids,
Kids where the quiet is,
Kids where the riot is –
Just like I said:
Fifty-seven varieties . . .

If you think about that lot
It'll drive you up the wall;
If you ask me, it's a miracle
The place works at all.

## Cloud Dragon

There's a dragon in the clouds:
Can't you see his open jaws?
And the spikes along his back?
And his twisty, crooked claws?
Look, he's changing shape now –
He's wider, not so tall:
Trying to fool us into thinking
He isn't there at all.
But be patient for a moment,
Just keep looking at the sky
And among the misty billows
That cloud dragon will come by.

## Just One Snag

Hooray, hooray
For the homework machine!
It's the greatest invention
That's ever been seen.

You just pop your school homework
Into the slot,
And it gulps and it burps
And flashes a lot.

Then from **OUTPUT** there comes,
On sheets clean and white,
Your homework – all done,
And everything's right!

There is just one snag
And it happened today:
I'd put nothing in,
But in the **OUT** tray

Was a sheet, with a heading
And questions below:
**TEST ON YOUR INPUTS –
TO SEE WHAT YOU KNOW.**

# After Snow

Just a few footprints in the snow:
Yours perhaps? I wouldn't know.
I'm certain that they are not mine.
First-footing in new snow is fine,
But waking to that dazzling white
After secret snow at night,
I'd wonder at a world new-minted
And leave perfection quite unprinted.

# An Alien Limerick

As on Red Planet, Mars, we alighted,
A very large banner we sighted.
'That's the answer,' I said,
'To why Mars is called "red".'
It said MARTIANS ALL LOVE MAN UNITED.

# Robin

In the stable where the Christ child lay
A small brown bird pecked in the hay.
The stable's fire was almost dead
And seeing this, the small bird spread
Its wings out by the last faint spark.
Then, fluttering like a meadowlark,
It fanned it once more into flame.
Good Joseph built the fire again.
Mary, smiling, blessed the bird.
Neither she nor Joseph heard
The bird's faint cries, and neither guessed
At the burnt feathers on its breast.

But when in God's good time new feathers came,
The robin's breast was red as any flame.

# Best-of-all Festival

At school the time that's best of all
Is when it's Harvest Festival.
There's fruit and veg and loads of flowers
To be arranged – it all takes hours.
Then we all go in to Assembly –
The hall's jam-packed – it's just like Wembley.
There's mums and dads and teachers there;
The vicar talks and says a prayer;
After the hymns our teacher comes
And lets us chat to dads and mums,
Then it's dinnertime – we've done no sums!

And after lunch, the great display
Is taken down and sent away
To the hospital nearby.
We all help – it makes time fly –
With packing up and making labels
And moving boxes, chairs and tables.
There's just no time to write or spell –
It's end of school, there goes the bell.

Oh yes, the best school day of all
Is when it's Harvest Festival.

# Haiku

Poem in three lines:
Five syllables, then seven,
Five again; no rhyme.

# Highcoo

Up on the ledges
Above the city traffic:
Fond sounds of pigeons.

# Hicuckoo!

Back again so soon?
Or is it just those mad boys
Fooling in the wood?

# Our Solar System

We made a model of the Solar System today
On our school field after lunch.
Sir chose nine of us
To be planets
And he parked the rest of the class
In the middle of the field
In a thoroughly messy bunch.
'You're the sun,' he brays,
'Big, huge; stick your arms out
In all directions
To show the sun's rays.'
The bit about sticking arms out
Really wasn't very wise
And I don't mind telling you
A few fingers and elbows
Got stuck in a few eyes.
Big Bill took a poke at Tony
And only narrowly missed him,
And altogether it looked
More like a shambles
Than the start of the Solar System.
The nine of us who were planets
Didn't get a lot of fun:
I was Mercury and I stood
Like a Charlie
Nearest of all to the sun
And all the sun crowd
Blew raspberries and shouted,
'This is the one we'll roast.
We're going to scorch you up, Titch,
You'll be like a black slice of toast!'

Katy was Venus and Val was Earth
And Neville Stephens was Mars
And the sun kids shouted and
Wanted to know
Could he spare them any of his Bars.
A big gap then to Jupiter (Jayne)
And a bigger one still to Saturn,
And Sir's excited and rambling on
About the System's mighty pattern.
'Now, a walloping space to Uranus,' he bawls,
'It's quite a bike away from the sun.'
Ha blooming ha — at least somebody here's
Having a whole load of fun.
He's got two planet kids left
And Karen's moaning
About having to walk so far:
She's Neptune — I suppose Sir's
Cracking some joke about
Doing X million miles by car.
Pete's Pluto — 'The farthest flung of all,'
Says Sir,
He's put by the hedge and rests,
But soon he starts picking blackberries
And poking at old birds' nests.
'Of course,' yells Sir, 'the scale's not right
But it'll give you
A rough idea.
Now when I blow my whistle
I want you all to start on your orbits —
Clear?'
Well, it wasn't of course,

And most of the class, well,
Their hearts weren't really in it,
Still, Sir's OK. So we gave it a go,
With me popping round the sun
About ten times a minute,
And Pluto on the hedge ambling round
Fit to finish his orbit next year.
We'd still have been there but
A kid came out of school and yelled,
'The bell's gone and the school bus's here!'
Well, the Solar System
Broke up pretty fast,
And my bus money had gone from my sock
And I had to borrow.
I suppose we'll have to draw diagrams
And write about it tomorrow.

# Ian Souter

Ian Souter is a teacher who lives in Australia. He has always loved playing about with the sounds, rhythm and rhyme of words as well as creating idiotic images in his brain. He doesn't have a dog to take for walks so he takes thoughts in his head instead.

He has a lovely wife and two children who look after him. They feed and dress him, as well as making sure he is not late for school! He also likes to stay fit so he tries to play football but his knees are not very keen on this idea. They can be heard cracking and creaking, then muttering, 'You're too old, you silly fool!'

## Dinosaur Diets

If a brontosaurus
ever stood before us,
it would simply explore us
and then – ignore us;
for in the stomach of a brontosaurus,
plants always came before us!

But if a tyrannosaurus
came across us,
ever saw us,
it would simply adore us;
for in the stomach of a tyrannosaurus
is where they liked to **store us**!

# My Grandpa

My grandpa is as round-shouldered
as a question mark
and is led about all day
by his walking stick.
With teeth that aren't real,
hidden behind a moustache that is,
while his memories simmer warmly
inside his crinkled paper bag of a face.

My grandpa,
old and worn on the outside,
sparky and fresh on the in.
For he often
shakes my hand with fifty-pence pieces,
makes sweets pop out from behind his ears,
smokes all day like a train
then laughs like one as well.
Plays jokes on my mother
as he tries to freshen her face with a smile
and then tells me stories that electrify my brain.

But best of all,
when my dad loses his temper,
Grandpa just tells him
*to sit down and behave himself!*

Good old Grandpa!

# I'm Coming to Get You!

Watch out,
I'm coming to get you –
Yes I am!
So go on, scat – run
Jump in your pram;
For I'll be sucking at your window
And getting ready to flow,
Then oozing while choosing
Which way I'll go!

So . . . watch out,
I'm coming to get you –
Yes I am!
No time to scream,
No time to scram;
For I'll be bubbling and squelching,
Slithering across the floor,
Spluttering and muttering
What I've got in store.

So . . . watch out,
I'm coming to get you –
Yes I am!
Push your door shut,
Even give it a slam,
For the lights will all be gone,
The dark switched on.
And there'll be nothing you can do
When I come after you!

But . . . you might have to wait a minute,
Well . . . just until I've drunk my hot chocolate,
And . . . just until I've brushed my teeth,
And . . . just until I'm in my Thomas the Tank pjs,
And oh . . . just until I find my spectacles,
For I'm just a little bit short-sighted,
But – when that's all done,
You're target number one.
So watch out,
This little brother of yours
is coming to get you!
**YES**
**I AM!!**

# Squirrel at the Bus Stop

My street is sharp with light
as trees blaze like fireworks
and above, the sun has spilled
a brilliant orange across the sky.
The morning has been up for hours
and is dazzled by autumn's colour.

As I drift past soundless houses
it appears that for a frozen moment
everything is still as a photograph
until a bustle of breeze hustles by
and trees begin their morning exercises,
bending and touching their toes,
while leaves pirouette around me
or dive to crunch themselves under my feet.

But suddenly I am halted by surprise
for there on the other side of the street
stands a squirrel waiting at a bus stop!
It is knee-deep in crisps of leaves
and looks worried with concern.
I muse that perhaps it has missed its bus
or perhaps it's even waiting for
some out-of-town squirrel to arrive
but a blur of speeding car
flashes rapidly between us
and, apparently, takes the squirrel with it!

Above, autumn's colours change
as the orange is wiped away
and the sun drops behind
a hedge of darkening cloud.
The morning is ageing now
so I hurry on towards the school
but that early morning light
still clings so warmly to my thoughts.

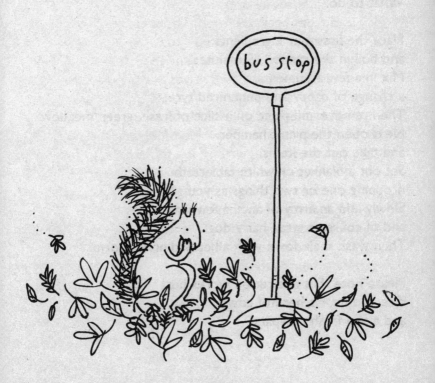

# Recipe for a Disastrous Family Picnic

Ingredients:

2 fed-up parents
1 crying baby
2 arguing children
1 picnic hamper full of sticky goodies
that will attract ants, wasps and hairy things!
1 unreliable car
1 green meadow

What to do:

Place the first four ingredients
and boil in the car for 45 minutes.
Mix in a few arguments,
a change of nappy and punctured tyre.
Then remove and place on a slice of fresh, green meadow.
Next open the picnic hamper
and take out the items.
Set out a blanket or white tablecloth
dropping one or two things as you go!
Slowly add an army of ants, a few wasps
and of course a stray, hairy dog!
Then wash it all down with a heavy thunderstorm.

Please note that this recipe works best
if served near a herd of cows
and a few fresh cowpats!

# Facing the Wrath

As the light deadens
the sea strengthens
like some great grizzly bear
with its powerful, rippling body
angrily clawing at the shore.

But a brave, small vessel
has dared to face the wrath
and aided by a fading sun,
whose final effort has been
to torch a path of light,
the lone boat turns from the shore.
Its blade of white sail
slices along the lit pathway
and, unbowed, heads out
towards the waiting horizon.

## The Word Is:

you can eat them
you can weigh them,
you can hang on them,
you can use one in jest,
you can pass one to the wise,
you can be as good as one,
you can place one in someone's ear,
you can take them right out of people's mouths,
you can have the last final one
and you can even be perfect with one.

But please don't take my word for it!

# Stepping into Space

clever

be

that

wouldn't

now

space,

into

stepping

imagine

just

But

ever.

for

on

and

on

go

can

that

stuff

boring

pretty

are

Stairs

# Nothing Can Get Me!

Sometimes when I'm all alone
in our lounge
with only the television
chatting to itself,
the dark arrives
to worry.

So then I scurry
to drag the curtains tight-closed
and hurry to disappear
inside our sofa.

I leap into its pink arms,
my legs swept high off the ground –
just in case –
and there I freeze
as the dark tries to squeeze
through a gap or crack
into the room.

Then I pile cushions
over feet,
over stomach,
over me
to huddle behind
and
cuddle behind
until I feel safe that
*nothing can get me!*

## Super Trouble!

Do you know Superman and Superwoman?
Well I do because I've got them
as parents – *Superparents!*
(That's my mum and dad to you!)

You see my parents happen to have these
really annoying,
really irritating,
really unbearable
and really unfair
super powers!

For example:

My dad has these X-ray eyes
that seem to know what I am thinking
before I actually think it.
Yesterday I heard, 'There'll be no sweets before tea.'
For goodness sake, he was in the next room
and I was only looking at the packet!

And he has this nose (it must be amplified!)
that can smell trouble anywhere, any place!
It's 'revenge time', you're creeping out
of your bedroom to dive-bomb your brother
when Dad's voice leaps largely up the stairs,
'And where do you think you're going, young man?'

Then there's Mum with her telescopic eyes
scanning, searching for the slightest sign of dirt.
Her radar goes berserk after football – Beep! Beep! **BEEP!!**
'Why are you covered in mud?'
'Well, I was the goalkeeper, Mum.'
'Well, next time stay away from the ball!'

And she's also got this amazing, extending neck
that allows her to be everywhere
and into everybody's else's business.
In fact if it was long enough I'm sure
she would stick it up the chimney as a periscope
and scan the whole neighbourhood!

Superparents, super powers, *super trouble!*

# Far Deadlier than the Male

Hi, the name's Cobra,
Jane Cobra.
A double agent;
a snake in the grass
or deadly assassin!
Also known as 00S, double O S (ssss)
and if in distress
I can be slippery and smooth-tongued
or I can twist *me* round your little finger (or neck!).
But then again,
I have a certain bite to my personality
and can transfix you with my hypnotic stare.
I'm trained to deal with poisoned pen letters
and, in my hooded disguise,
can easily slip in and out of secret places.
But be warned not to forge a friendship
or bond
for I'm cold-blooded
and never feel any fangs of regret!

At the end of the day –
I like nothing better than
a simple game of snakes and ladders,
a Martini, squeezed but not shaken,
and to slip from my skin
into something . . . sssssmoother!

Cobra, Jane Cobra's the name,
far deadlier than the male of the species!

# After the Match

The football match is over, the game lost
and I stumble through the Saturday crowd
chasing my father's energetic steps.
We head for the welcome of home,
struggling along lonely, dismal streets
where an uneasy feeling of guilt surrounds us
as lampposts glare angrily down
and faceless windows stare coldly out.

Now far into dark corners
shadows begin to twitch
and a growl of distant cars –
hunting in a pack –
roars off into the night.
Suddenly a scream of brakes
yells harshly over our heads
but nothing reacts apart from my fears
which, as one, duck inside my head.
Swiftly I grab for the safety of my father's hand
where fingers reach for fingers,
hand closes knowingly on hand
until I gaze upwardly searching
the added security of my father's face,
only to realize that he has become
a stranger!

# The Kitchen Work-Out

On top of a work surface
a loud-mouthed radio
is shouting relentlessly,
'Come on, you lot,
you're not switched on this morning.
Shocking attitude!'

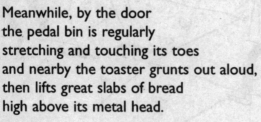

Immediately, the washing machine
has a burst of energy
and starts performing forward rolls,
while inside the microwave
a plate of sausages sprint speedily
around their glass track,
running out of their skins
until they collapse exhausted
at the final 'ping'.

Meanwhile, by the door
the pedal bin is regularly
stretching and touching its toes
and nearby the toaster grunts out aloud,
then lifts great slabs of bread
high above its metal head.

Standing in the corner
the kettle has now run out of steam
dehydrated and desperately in need of water,
while across the room in the kitchen bowl
cups and plates practise lengths
across greasy, murky water.
Unfortunately, a lone cereal bowl
has gathered the wooden spoon
and suddenly experiences a sinking feeling.

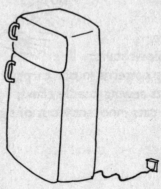

Only the refrigerator,
white-faced and unmoved,
refuses to join in;
quietly chuckling in the corner
and just practising at being Mr Cool.

## Scat Cat

Our cat
skims across floors
spins round corners
chasing its own tail;
a blur of ebony fur.

Our cat
scats downstairs,
ripping patterns in our carpet
with its sewing needle claws;
pitter pats innocently out of sight.

Our cat
drags a feathered sack of bird
into the kitchen
then stalks the garden;
freezing everything that moves.

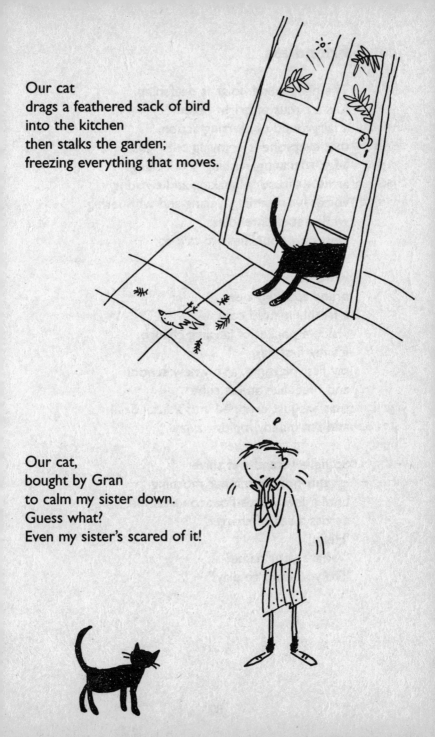

Our cat,
bought by Gran
to calm my sister down.
Guess what?
Even my sister's scared of it!

## Friendless

The playground noise is deafening.
It is a circus of bright colour;
a fairground of blurring action
that everyone is enjoying but – me!
Legs – running, rushing and kicking,
arms – thrusting, shaking and twisting,
voices – screaming, yelling and whispering
while I stand friendless,
with only Loneliness to talk to.

Here I am,
brand spanking new;
a freshly minted coin
inside a pocket of jangling change.
It's my first day,
my first playtime, at my new school
and I feel like an ice cube
that has just dropped into a fizzy drink
and I'm quietly melting away.

So here I stand and shiver
on this hot September morning
until a few words float towards me
across a sea of chatter.
'Hello!'
'What's your name?'
'Do you want to play?'

Suddenly it's not me any more it's we!
I have been welcomed into the action.
So, as a smile slowly spreads inside my mouth,
I cross the playground
and join in their game,
leaving Loneliness in the shadows
to play on its own.

## Sports Day

Now you mustn't worry
it won't be like last year,
this time I'm prepared
even got all the gear!

I know last Sports Day
there was a bit of an alarm
but I couldn't help falling
and breaking my arm!

Now you must understand
the family pride is at stake
but this time — no slip-up,
trip-up or silly mistake.

Yes, I've done all the sweating,
I've *even* lost weight
just stand back and watch me
as I take off — accelerate.

So off to the finish,
and look out for the first place,
for it's time for me to take part
in the annual Father's Race!

# My Dad's Amazing

My dad's *amazing* for he can:

make mountains out of molehills,
teach Granny to suck eggs,
make Mum's blood boil
and then drive her up the wall.

My dad's *amazing* for he also:

walks around with his head in the clouds,
has my sister eating out of his hand,
says he's got eyes in the back of his head
and can read me like a book.

But,
the most *amazing* thing of all is:

when he's caught someone red-handed
first he jumps down their throat
and then he bites their head off!

# The World Widens

Red! Amber! Green!
Traffic lights wave us on
until we are squeezing along streets
where inquisitive houses lean forward
and sleeping policemen step out boldly
to slow our progress.

Eventually the world widens
and we are flashing by shop fronts
where frozen models offer the latest fashions
and loud posters announce the latest sales.
Alongside us now a train jogs out
from under a red-bricked bridge;
it coughs several times then sprints off
towards some distant destination.

Now as we accelerate towards home
street lights slowly flicker awake
and rows of dulled catseyes
energetically snap open,
while the purring breath of night
whispers darkly in our slipstream.

## Answers from p34

TADPOLE

PLANET EARTH

ICICLE
SNOWFLAKE
FOG

DANDELION CLOCK

RULER

FIGURE 8